DROPLET
THE POWER OF WATER

YASHASVI BULUSU

BLUEROSE PUBLISHERS
India | U.K.

Copyright © Yashasvi Bulusu 2023

All rights reserved by author. No part of this publication may be reproduced, stored in a retrieval system or transmitted in any form or by any means, electronic, mechanical, photocopying, recording or otherwise, without the prior permission of the author. Although every precaution has been taken to verify the accuracy of the information contained herein, the publisher assume no responsibility for any errors or omissions. No liability is assumed for damages that may result from the use of information contained within.

BlueRose Publishers takes no responsibility for any damages, losses, or liabilities that may arise from the use or misuse of the information, products, or services provided in this publication.

For permissions requests or inquiries regarding this publication,
please contact:

BLUEROSE PUBLISHERS
www.BlueRoseONE.com
info@bluerosepublishers.com
+91 8882 898 898
+4407342408967

ISBN: 978-93-93385-19-2

Printed in INDIA

Cover design: Aman Sharma
Typesetting: Namrata Saini

First Edition: June 2023

Acknowledgement

I am extremely grateful to my parents who had complete faith in me and supported me all the way up to the completion of my book. Special thanks to my mother for her guidance and critical analysis throughout the write up.

My sincere gratitude to my Principal Madam, Mrs. Sangeeta Uppal, my Co-ordinator, Mrs Jyoti Hirpathak and Mrs. Meenakshi Sharma, my class teacher for their support and encouragement.

Foreword 1

I am delighted and honoured to write the foreword for this remarkable book, 'Droplet- The power of water,' by young talented author Yashasvi Bulusu of The Millennium School, Indore.

Yashasvi is a unique kid whom I have known for the past couple of years. His penchant for books is amazing and one may find his knowledge in art of story weaving well-articulated in the book 'Droplet- The power of water.' The tale carries a beautiful message for humanity.

Superheroes are every kid's fantasy and imagination. In this book, Yashasvi has created this delightful character TISVA- who is searching for his father. One falls in love with the protagonist immediately. The book is a thrilling tale of action, heroism, and power of valour when one faces adversity. It also shares a special bond between a father and his son.

This Sci-Fi book, 'Droplet' will, like a magnet, draw young kids to read it over and over again. The effort of a budding author is to be applauded for drafting an excellent novel for kids where you will immerse in an exciting journey.

So, get ready to be a part of an amazing adventure, which you will not forget soon.

Happy Reading..!!!!!!!!!

Mrs. Sangeeta Uppal

Principal

The Millennium School, Indore.

Eminent educationist from the past 32 years.

Recipient of Sandipani Vasishta Gurujan Samman 2010.

Awarded as most effective Principal by AKS

Foreword 2

Every day I see people doing great things in the world. What do they have in common? The courage to go after their dreams and make a positive impact. I have known Yashasvi Bulusu as a small boy and an innocent learner stepping ahead as a teenager. His academic growth and imaginative potential were anticipated.

Droplet is about Tisva's journey and transformation from a childish boy to a strong and mature person. I can foresee the transfiguration of the author. Tisva's search for his father leads to learning of panchatattva and mastering Apa Vidya. The protagonist masters the art of controlling water [Apa vidya] for spreading happiness, goodness, and defeating the bad. He teaches us the motive of facing life and truth with courage, love, and kindness instead of fear.

Wishing all the luck and happiness.
Mrs. Jyoti Hirpathak
Coordinator and facilitator
TMS Indore

Contents

Chapter 1: Tisva 1

Chapter 2: Pancha Tattva 4

Chapter 3: Apa Vidya 7

Chapter 4: The lost ring 10

Chapter 5: Secrets of Aither 14

Chapter 6: Crisis I 17

Chapter 7: It is my birthday 20

Chapter 8: Crisis II 24

Chapter 9: Power Of Water 29

Chapter 10: Droplet 32

Chapter 11: Superhero 37

Glossary 40

Chapter 1

TISVA

Tisva was never a morning bird. However, he woke up early and got ready for school. Sarita uttered shockingly, "Oh! my dear son. Are you well? What happened to you today?" He answered, "Mom, I am very much fine, do not worry, I just want to go to school early today." As he was getting fresh, he suddenly looked up at his grandparents and was surprised. They had bought a new bag for him. He was overly excited for he knew that it was a gift for his 14th birthday just two days away. He did need a new bag as his old one was torn. Excitedly he said, "Oh my god! A new bag from my favorite company, The Blue Stars, THANK YOU!!" He ate his breakfast quickly and took the bus to school. As he left, he waved to his mother. "Take care, bye," said Sarita.

(In the bus.)

"Tisva, we all have a father, but your father is missing, why?" asked a concerned Chandu. Chandu was Tisva's friend. Tisva gazed outside the window and said, "This is a mystery, nobody knows where he is and whether he is even alive or dead" said Tisva sadly. He continued, "I feel very sad but one day I promise I'll find my dad." As they were talking, something magical happened! Suddenly, everyone on the bus started to disappear, including his friend Chandu too! Tisva was startled as the bus was moving automatically. Suddenly something appeared in front of the bus. It was going in circles and sucking up everything like it was a portal. The bus was moving fast and into the portal and ………………… whoosh.

Tisva found himself on the grass near a lake. He stood up, scratching his head, confused, and wondering, "Aah, what a beautiful place! But what is this place? Where am I?" There was a lake with clear fresh water. Some ducks were swimming and birds were playing on the surface of the water. He also saw green trees with colorful flowers. The sky was very pretty with fluffy clouds. Then, he saw a huge building, more like a mansion but it looked old. Above the mansion, he saw something flying swiftly. It was a big bird. The bird landed and Tisva was surprised to see a man sitting on the bird. The man wore a peculiar purple suit with a blue-striped tie. As he got down the bird, Tisva asked, "Hello mister, who are you? Where am I? The man funnily questioned back "Don't you know me?" Tisva nodded "No." The man again said, "You really don't know MEEEE?" As Tisva looked at him puzzled, he said, "My name is Danu, I am your father's friend." "What! How can you be my father's friend? You do not joke with me because I am not a child. I will be fourteen in two days" said Tisva angrily. Instantly Danu remarked, "So rude, your father was never like this." Tisva was stunned and asked, "Do you even know my father?!" Then, Danu replied, "Yes, I know him very well!" Now, Tisva was frozen. He requested Danu to tell him about his father, but Danu told him that he would find out about his father only when he was capable enough to understand. Tisva snapped, "Understand what!" Danu told the young boy that he had to first understand and learn about the five elements of nature and how to control water. Danu explained that the mansion in front of them was a university called Pancha-tattva-eka where students learn about the elements of life which are water, fire, earth, air, and sky. Tisva had to first gain the knowledge of Pancha tattva and master the art of controlling water called 'Apa vidya.' Now, Tisva was getting impatient and said, "But why! Why do I have to learn this Apa vidya and blah blah." Without answering his childish questions, Danu walked towards the building as Tisva rushed restlessly behind him.

Chapter 2

PANCHA TATTVA

A bewildered Tisva was murmuring to himself, "Somebody help! Mamma, please take me home, oh, where am I stuck?" and he walked towards the mansion. The mansion was gigantic and surrounded by four pillars. There was something strange about the pillars. They were disappearing. Danu shouted, "Come quickly! Enter the mansion before it disappears otherwise, you will be stuck here." Tisva ran and entered the mansion.

He was amazed at what he saw inside Pancha-tattva-eka. The place was much larger on the inside than it appeared on the outside. It was magical. There were five majestic palaces inside. The place was picturesque. It was full of greenery. There were plenty of colorful and fragrant flowers. Tisva also saw many shimmering springs and streams with gorgeous swans swimming in the water. Many birds and butterflies were hovering around the place. Far Behind, there were mountains covered with silvery snowcaps. It was a splendid view. Indeed mesmerizing. There were many young boys and girls walking around. Some were playing with fire. Some more were juggling with balls of water while others were flying in the air. Suddenly, Tisva realized that Danu was not present there.

After a while, a young man came and said, "Hello Tisva, I am a helper from Apa Vidyalaya. The sun is going to set soon, come for dinner." The young man escorted Tisva to the dining room which was huge. There too, were many students. Tisva silently ate his dinner. Afterward, the helper took him to his room. Tisva was very curious about the place. So, he asked the helper, "Please tell me about this beautiful place." The young man started talking, "This is the magnificent city of 'Aither.' The mightiest god Eka created it. Aither is a personification of the universe and heaven, a place where gods reside. It was made of the Panchatattva or the five elements, which are Apa- the water, Agni- the fire, then Prithvi- the earth, Anil- the air, and Akasha- the sky. The five palaces in the Aither city represent each of the elements. " Finally, he said, "We shall meet tomorrow again…. My name is Vapih. Do remember me!" and bid goodnight.

It was too late in the night, Tisva was very tired. He lay down on the bed in his new room and was lost in his thoughts. He was tossing on his bed and remembering home. "Mother would be worried," he said to himself. Sometime later he slept off. The next morning, he woke up early and scanned his room. He was surprised at what he saw. He had his own study table and a book rack. There were clothes and shoes, all of them fitting his size. There was a particular costume with a unique droplet symbol. It was light blue in color with dark cobalt blue shoes matching it. It might be the uniform, he thought. Tisva got ready and went down to the dining hall for breakfast. After breakfast, he had to meet his principal.

Chapter 3

APA VIDYA

At the office, there was a long queue waiting for the principal. All the while he was only worried about his mother. At last, he met the principal. The man had a charming personality. He looked to be centuries old but was very active. With a pleasant smile, he greeted, "Good morning Tisva, my boy. We are very glad to finally meet you here. My name is Tattva-eka." Immediately Tisva uttered, "Sir, I am worried about my mother, she does not know where I am." The old man smiled, put his hands around the boy, and told him, "Son, your mother is not worried, so, you too should not worry." Still, Tisva innocently insisted, "No, she must be worried because I am not at home." Sir Tattva-eka explained that time in the city of Aither was faster than the time in the world on the other side of the portal. On hearing this, Tisva became speechless and stared at him. He also promised Tisva that once he completed his training, he would return to the same time and place from where he vanished from his world. Tisva was still unclear and asked, "But! How can this be possible?" The learned person explained to him that the rhythm or laya of time worked in a unique way in Aither. "You will soon understand my boy, but for now concentrate on your training and master Apa vidya" he assured Tisva.

(Outside the office) A patient Vapih was waiting for Tisva. He accompanied him to the nearby stream and instructed him to juggle with water, to which Tisva snapped, "Wait, what! juggle with water? Do I look like a magician?" Somebody spoke from behind, "It is not magic! it is the art of communicating with nature and controlling it." Vapih informed, "Look around, your teacher has come!" Tisva turned around and saw Danu. He shouted, "So, you are my teacher, Danu sir!"

Sir Danu was the professor of Apa Vidyalaya. He mastered the art of Apa vidya. He explained, "Tisva, you have a strong connection with the energy of water. You must focus and connect with that energy to master it." He added, "In nature, water is pure, serene, and ever-flowing. Its energy is free and has no limits. So, you need to respect it to control it. It even has both healing and destructive powers. So, you must use it wisely. Start your practice, my boy, you have a long day to go. Vapih will be watching you."

With his hands on his waist, Tisva gasped. He took a deep breath. Unaware of where to start, Tisva started splashing water. Vapih was smiling calmly. Tisva was annoyed with him. He said, "Do you think it is a cakewalk!? Can you juggle with water? Without answering him, Vapih took little water in his palm, made three balls from it, and juggled. Tisva was shocked. Vapih then merged the three water balls and made one large ball. Tisva wanted to hold the ball and asked for it. As soon as he held the ball, it burst in his hands and the water splashed on his face. He got upset. He then requested Vapih,

"Please, will you teach me?" Vapih agreed and both started playing in the stream. At least now, Tisva made a new friend.

It was already noon, Tisva was hungry, and they both went to the lunch hall. Upon reaching, he requested Vapih to have lunch with him. As they both started eating, he realized that Vapih ate very less as compared to him. Tisva enquired, "You eat so less. Aren't you feeling hungry? We were playing in the sun for such a long time!" Vapih replied, "My friend, with regular dhyana and pranayama I get Ojas or energy that is why I feel less hungry."

After lunch, they spent the remaining day playing with water and chatting with each other. At night, Vapih gave Tisva his training and study schedules. It included training with water, pranayama, meditation, mudra practice, and study of all the five elements. Even after one month, Tisva could not connect with water. However, with regular pranayama and dhyana, he became calm. Vapih helped Tisva in his studies too. They both became best buddies.

Chapter 4

THE LOST RING

Three months passed away. Tisva became more mature. One peaceful and pleasant morning, like every day, Tisva started his training. While splashing the water in the air he saw water forming different shapes and flying from his hands. He shouted in excitement, "Hurray! I have done it!" Vapih was glad for him and congratulated him. That day, during lunch, in spite of a very hectic day, he ate less food as he was not very hungry. Instantly, he remembered what Vapih told him. He realized that his energy must have increased. The next morning, Danu paid a visit to his pupil. He was awe-struck as his young learner could now control water and make various kinds of shapes with it. Tisva was delighted, he asked Danu if he had permission to go back to his world and meet his mother and grandparents. Danu smiled and told him that it was only the beginning. There was much more to learn. In spite of being sad, Tisva agreed to continue training with the five elements. Thereafter, Danu told him that he was now ready to learn more about Aither. He said, "Today I will tell you the story of the lost ring." Tisva sat down enthusiastically to hear the story.

Danu started his narration, "Listen, many years ago, there were three beloved students who studied at Pancha-tattva-eka University. They were mighty, valiant, powerful, and divine. They spent many years to understand and master the Pancha tattva of life." Tisva remarked, "It seems to be a true story.

What were their names?" Danu answered, "They were Dhruthi, Ravi, and Samudra." Danu paused a little and was lost in thoughts. He continued, "They were my friends. Samudra and I trained Apa Vidya together. He was robust, strongest, the most powerful and divine from birth. Dhruti was a personification of purity, beauty, and humility. She was an honest, spiritual, and yet powerful warrior of Aither. Ravi was as powerful as the sun. He had all the qualities of the sun's energy. He was an essence of brightness, justice, and valor just like a king." As Danu spoke, he was very gratified. Tisva was listening to every word with his wide-open eyes. Then Danu became serious and said, "However, there was a fierce warrior. He was almost as powerful as Eka. He was Samudra. He was deep, powerful, and divine at the same time, but he was proud and greedy too."

Nevertheless, they were favorites of all the teachers. They had one major task, to protect the world. Once, Eka held a competition to find out the most capable warrior. All the warriors of Aither took part in the competition. Everyone assumed that Samudra would be the winner. However, Eka was impressed with Ravi and Dhruti. He was most impressed with the virtues of Ravi and gifted him a divine ring. Ravi was made divine and given powers to create and protect life. At the same time, Dhruthi too was blessed by Eka who made her divine just like Ravi. However, Samudra was not happy. He became greedy. He was jealous of Ravi and tried to steal the ring from Ravi. Thereafter, Samudra challenged Ravi and Dhruti. An intense battle took place. Wickedly, Samudra misused nature and fought immorally. Ravi and Dhruti were concerned about the ring. If Samudra got the divine ring it would be extremely dangerous. They even tricked Samudra, but he was one step ahead. So, in the confusion, the ring was lost.

Finally, Ravi and Dhruti surrendered to Samudra as they could not find the ring. Samudra was furious. Eka banished and prohibited Samudra from entering the Pancha-tattva-eka University. Samudra retreated to the depths of the sea. He captured his two friends and put them in the dungeons. Tisva gasped, "So, no one knows where the ring is! Did the other warriors not search for it?" Danu looked optimistically into his eyes and spoke, "Yes, they searched for it, but nobody could find the divine ring. We hope, someday, somewhere, and sometime it will definitely be found."

Tisva was puzzled with the way his teacher looked at him. However, he understood that there was much more to the story than what he learnt. For the time, he felt happy that he was making progress. He was also determined to find out the entire truth.

Chapter 5

SECRETS OF AITHER

Generally, the days of Aither city were always pleasant and cheerful, and nights were cold and misty. However, that day, the mist on the mountains did not descend. Clouds covered the sun, and one could still feel the night chill. "Hmm, today the weather feels unusual," said Tisva. Suddenly the water of the streams and springs turned turbulent. Vapih stood up to check the water and shouted, "Tisva, come fast. We must go to our shelter." Tisva was puzzled. He noticed fish floating in the water as they were dead. He cried, "Oh no! Are the fish dead?" He saw many students running to take shelter. Vapih and Tisva went into their room and locked the door.

As they both looked outside the window, they saw many warriors around the city. Tisva asked, "what is happening?" Vapih told him that it was an attack! He told them not to worry because the warriors would protect them all. Tisva pondered, "Could it be Samudra behind the attack?" Then, abruptly the skies turned dark, and the stars appeared. Immediately Vapih instructed Tisva to take back his hands from the window. He closed all the windows. Tisva was shaken and asked, "Please explain me, what is happening?" His friend told him that the warriors were laying down protective measures for the safety of Pancha-tattva-eka University. Vapih said, "Tisva, Time is unique, if someone is working hard and is busy, time appears to pass extremely fast. If one is lazy, time is slow. You see, it is a relative dimension. Laya is a divine and mystic warrior here, who can alter time, its rhythm, and speed. She is capable of changing the rhythm of anything to protect this city and the world. She has hastened our time, which is why it is night now. Also, Pancha-tattva-eka must have vanished from its location. Whenever there is a possibility of an attack like today, it keeps changing its location randomly. Pancha-tattva-eka radiates energy to its surroundings. Whenever night falls this energy decreases making it difficult to trace the city. Also, the energy shields must have been increased. We cannot go out anywhere." "Did laya put up the shields?" enquired Tisva. Vapih told him that Commander Ojas created the energy shields. "Ojas is a vibrant and divine warrior. He was made the commander of security by Eka. He gains his energy from the sun and moon. He must have spread protective shields all around," answered Vapih. Tisva exclaimed, "Wow, all of this sounds so mysterious. Wait, why cannot we call Eka to help us? He is the mightiest, is he not?" "You are right, he is the mightiest god. He was the first teacher at this university. He built and expanded it very patiently. We are always grateful to him. However, right now, he will not come, he is hurt and away doing his penance. Nevertheless, if our warriors need help, he will know telepathically and he will come to protect them. He is hurt because of his son Samudra. Many years ago, Samudra destroyed our beautiful city and captured two of our very bold warriors. You very well know what he did to Aither."

informed Vapih. Tisva remembered the story narrated by his teacher Danu. Later on, Vapih told him that everything was under control.

The next morning, everything was again fresh and filled with life. As Vapih assured, everything was back to normal. Tisva was overjoyed to see all the fish alive and swimming. He exclaimed, "Hey, look at the fish! How did it happen?" "It is the duty of Piyusha the enchanted warrior to ensure that everything is always alive. She is the elixir of life. Nobody dies till she is around," said Danu as he came to check on his student. Danu explained that there is a gem named Pancha-ratna hidden in the grounds of Aither. It was planted by Eka and was a source of purity and harmony in life. It ensured the balance of the world. It is the most powerful gem in the world.

Chapter 6

CRISIS I

Days passed, months passed, and the security of Pancha-tattva-eka had become much tighter. Tisva was anxious to know who tried to attack. He thought, "Obviously, someone must have found out who attacked us." He wanted to know more about the precious stone as well as Laya, Piyusha, Ojas, and others. By now, he could roughly understand that Danu, Samudra, Dhruti, Ravi, and all the other warriors were from the same time. As he was lost in his thoughts, he walked straight into the stream and fell. He was completely soaked. The fish swarmed around him and started leaping over him like they wanted to play. Just then, Vapih extended his hand and pulled him out. The boys shared a laugh together. There, Danu was standing and could not stop smiling. Tisva ran to him and greeted him, "Good morning sir, will you tell me more about all the warriors of Aither." Danu nodded and said, "Okay, first change your clothes and meet me in my room."

Last time, when Danu narrated the lost ring, there were many facts he did not tell Tisva. So, he decided to reveal all the details. "Now, you have learned about my friends, Laya, Ojas, and Piyusha. All of them including Dhruti, Ravi, and Samudra were my friends. That day, when Samudra wanted to steal the divine ring, we all supported Dhruthi and Ravi in the fight against him. Samudra thought I would be on his side as we were best friends. I knew he was wrong so; I did not support him. That made him even angrier. I used my Apa Vidya on him, but he was the greatest warrior of Apa Vidya. I was no match for him. He used the destructive power of water and destroyed everything that came his way. We fought with valor, but he overpowered us. Then Laya suggested that Ravi and Dhruti should hide the ring. All of us could telepathically communicate with each other. Piyusha, Dhruti, and Ravi left the city through a portal. Laya, Ojas, and I assured them that we would follow them once we tackled Samudra. However, Samudra was cleverer. He understood our plans and pursued us. Meanwhile, our friends were looking for a place to hide the ring. It was a beautiful droplet shaped pearl ring. Eka encased all his great virtues into it. Though Samudra was Eka's beloved son, he was disobedient. He always took advantage of his divinity.

Ojas, the lord of energy, had a supreme gift of sensing all energies. He could feel Samudra was close by. It was raining heavily with thunderstorms. The sky was filled with thick and dark clouds. His presence made the rain even more terrifying. As he walked, huge waves of water washed away everything in the way. We had to divert Samudra's attention. So, I fought with him face to face again. Laya created a time loop and locked both of us inside it. she created multiple illusions and also changed the pattern of the wind to reduce its intensity. Ojas then used the energy of the lightning and created an energy shield around them for protection.

once the protection shield was laid around, Dhruti said, "Ravi, it is time we hide the divinity of the ring in the purest creation of life." Then, they transformed the ring into a beautiful baby. The ring itself disappeared as it took the form of an innocent child. Thereafter, Piyusha blessed the child with the elixir of life. Indeed, the baby was blessed with Eka's virtues.

I could no longer hold Samudra. The time loop broke and a huge wave of water lashed the energy shield too. It pushed away the baby and we lost the child. Alas! Laya's illusion on Samudra worked. We were successful. Samudra had no idea about the child. He searched for the ring everywhere but could not find it. He captured Ravi and Dhruti.

Eka was angry. However, he knew that the baby was safe. He spoke, "Destiny has more mysteries to come. Samudra has lost his right to be my son." He not only punished Samudra but also banished him from Aither. He believed that someday he would be taught a lesson," concluded Danu.

… Chapter 7

IT IS MY BIRTHDAY

At last, Tisva got permission to go home and celebrate his birthday. He was thrilled. He asked Vapih to accompany him. Vapih agreed to go. Tisva did not know, but Vapih was already instructed to go along with him. Danu told Vapih that it was for the boy's security. Vapih told Tisva that he would visit him at home by evening. Danu created the portal for Tisva to go to his world.

As he stepped into the portal, he found himself sitting in the bus next to his friend Chandu. All his school friends were chatting and laughing. It was unbelievable. He spent one full year training Apa Vidya, but he was back to the same moment he vanished. That day at school he found everything amazingly easy. All his teachers appreciated him for his work. He was the star of the class. After school, he took the bus to go home. He wondered to himself whether everything about his training, Pancha-tattva-eka, Vapih and everything else was a dream.

The bus approached his house. From a distance, he saw his mother on the terrace and was overjoyed. He shouted,

"Mother, I am home!" When the bus stopped, he hurriedly ran down the bus. Tisva lived in a cozy house in the middle of the fields. The house had a beautiful flower garden in the front yard. At the back, there was a vegetable garden. The house was surrounded by a picket fence. Tisva's grandfather used to be a farmer and his grandmother had been a homemaker. Sarita was always an independent lady. she worked as a teacher in the nearby school. Tisva opened the main gate of his house. He was delighted to see his grandfather. Grandpa wore his usual cap and was seated on his rocking chair reading the newspaper. He always enjoyed smoking from his pipe. His walking stick was lying next to the chair. Tisva ran and hugged him. Then he went up to the main door. It was open. His grandma was in the kitchen. After hugging her, he rushed up to the terrace to meet his mom. He held her tightly and cried, "Mom, you are the best! I love you! I missed you so much!" Sarita laughed and joked, "Oh really! You have been away only for a few hours. Come now, freshen up and eat something, you must be hungry." Tisva went to his room. He was ashamed to see his room untidy. At Aither, Vapih taught him how to clean his room and be disciplined. He immediately tidied his room and got fresh. Then, suddenly the doorbell rang. Tisva ran to open the door, "Vapih, it is you! I was waiting for you for a long time." He introduced Vapih to his family. Sarita remarked, "I never saw him earlier. Is he your new friend?" "Yes mother, he is my senior from school, and he helps me in my studies. I invited him to stay with us for a few days. Please allow him to stay." Sarita said that he was welcome. She served snacks to both boys.

The next day was a Sunday. Both the boys spent talking and enjoying in the fields. Tisva introduced Vapih to all his friends. They played all the day. At night Vapih reminded, "Tisva, after your birthday you have to return to Panchatattvaeka to finish your training. Tisva got a little upset but was happy that he was going to celebrate his birthday with his dear family. The next day, he got up early and got ready for school. Sarita and Vapih gave him birthday wishes and his grandparents blessed him. In the evening, there was a wonderful party. Tisva enjoyed it fully.

At night he decided to spend some time with his mother. He asked her, "Mother, please tell me about my father. Where is he?" Sarita looked at him warmly. She knew that she could not hide his secret any longer. She said, "Dear son, I am not your real mother. Fourteen years ago, I found you on the farms.

You were covered with a soft satin cloth inside a basket. Somebody left you." Tisva started crying. Sarita hugged him and said, "Son, don't cry, you will always be my dearest." She mentioned that his grandfather searched around to find any clues but could not find anything. We also wondered how you survived the huge thunderstorm from the previous night. Tisva returned to his room. He was silent. He narrated the whole story to Vapih, but Vapih did not look surprised. Vapih only assured him that his family loved him.

The next day, Tisva was told that they would be staying at home for a few more days. Tisva was excited and asked, "Did Sir extend my leave? Vapih nodded and replied, "No, there is another attack on Panchatattvaeka. To be safe we must stay here till further instructions."

Chapter 8

CRISIS II

While Tisva was busy celebrating his birthday, back at Aither, the rainy season began. Normally, it rained during the day and cleared up at night. That day, there was a downpour. The sky was filled with low-lying thick rain clouds. The rain continued even at night. Three days passed by, and there was no sun. It was wet and cold everywhere and no one could go out. All streams and rivers were flooding. This was very unusual. All the seasons in the city of Aither were always balanced. Tattva-eka, the principal stepped out in the rain to check the situation. He noticed that the fish grew large and wild. They instantaneously attacked him. However, using his Prithvi vidya he calmed them and saved himself. The situation was scary. "Why are the fish behaving so strangely? They all have grown so robust in the rain," Danu said. The principal remarked, "The balance of Aither is disturbed, there is an increase in the water element." As all the warriors got alerted, they saw the flood water turn into huge waves. Samudra emerged from inside the waves.

After Samudra was banished, he wanted to take revenge. He wanted to become the king of Aither. All these years, he prepared for war. He trained all the sea animals and made an army of them. Finally, Samudra successfully entered Panchatattvaeka. He was robust, gigantic and wore a golden armor. With a heavy and scary voice, he announced, "None of you is strong enough to fight me. So, do not waste your energy. Accept me as your master, otherwise, there will be a lot of destruction." He continued, "You will be able to live peacefully if you accept me."

Tattva-eka telepathically communicated with Eka, "Great master, we need your help." Eka responded, "Tattva-eka, I am unable to help. Many years ago, I promised Samudra that I would never hurt him or fight against him. I was blinded by love. I did not foresee the future. It was a mistake." Tattva-eka said, "Then please guide us." "You have a more important task to do now. Finish Tisva's training. He will bring balance." Said Eka. He continued, "Trust my words, the boy is capable of fighting and defeating Samudra. He was born out of the divine ring and has all my virtues. When he was created, he even absorbed the powers of all the warriors present around him. He only needs guidance. Danu will have to prepare the boy finally. Tisva must master the POWER OF WATER."

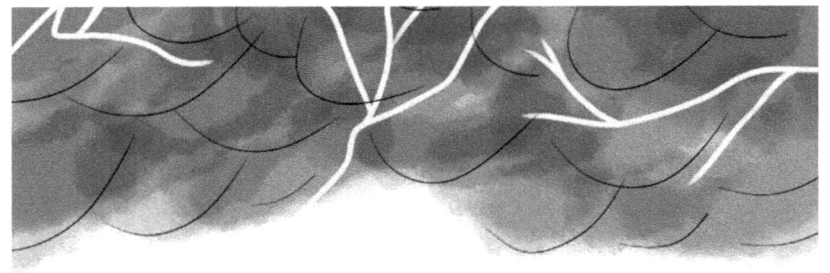

Being the principal, Tattva-eka agreed to Samudra's terms. He instructed all the warriors to accept Samudra as the new king. The warriors were not pleased but had faith in their principal. No one questioned Tattva-eka. They were patiently waiting for further instructions. They knew that if they revolted, they would be prisoned. However, there was something warriors were happy about. Ravi and Dhruthi were back in Aither, but they were still prisoners.

Samudra often wondered why the warriors surrendered without any fight. He said to himself, "They all are ants in front of me. He changed all the rules and safety measures of Pancha-tattva-eka. Nobody was allowed to open the portals to connect with the outside world.

Days passed, but the rain did not stop. The city continued to be wet and cold. Everyone adjusted to the unfamiliar environment. All the warriors continued the routine work during the day. At night they secretly worked on sharpening their energy and skills.

Day by day Samudra became more arrogant, unjust, and overconfident. His lifestyle was very lavish. His men used to party every night. Over time they became relaxed and careless. One day, Tattva-eka met Danu and said, "It is the appropriate time, we must use it to complete Tisva's training. You must immediately teleport to him. Danu promptly replied, "Yes sir, I shall definitely do so tonight."

Meanwhile, in the common man's world, Vapih and Tisva were eagerly waiting. During the day, they would go to school like normal kids. At night Tisva would continue his training. At times they would meditate for hours. Tisva's grandparents often complimented him that he had now become a mature and quieter kid, who was growing stronger day by day. Sarita was happy with Vapih staying around, as she felt he made Tisva a better person.

Chapter 9

POWER OF WATER

One night, the boys finished their training and slept off. Tisva was suddenly woken up by a dream. Vapih was already awake. "Hey! I dreamt that Danu Sir will be arriving tonight. I felt that he woke me up." Said Tisva. Vapih laughed and said, "You, silly boy! it was not a dream, but is true." "So, you mean it was a communication? Can I now telepathically receive messages?" Asked an astonished Tisva. Vapih (still laughing) said, "You could always telepathically communicate, you never realized it, dumbo."

As they were talking, Danu walked out of a portal, "Aah! So nice to see you boys! Vapih, you have done a great job. Tisva, you must finish learning the power of water," said Danu hurriedly. Tisva cooly said, "Okay, but why the hurry?" Danu told him, how Samudra captured Pancha-tattva-eka and that only he was capable of defeating Samudra. Tisva shockingly said, "No, no, I cannot defeat Samudra. He is a huge guy."

Danu had very less time. He said, "Listen, my boy, let me tell you about the origins of Pancha tattva and the power of water." He started his lesson, "Om is a sacred word. It is considered as the vibration and sound of the universe. The Panchatattva were born out of this primordial sound. They emerged out of Om in the following order- Shoonya/Akasha -Anil/Vayu -Anal/Agni -Apa/Jal-Prithvi. These five elements in their respective proportions form the entire creation in the world. The Apa tattva makes up the maximum percentage. When it is balanced it is pure, calm, healing, and free flowing. It even represents our emotions. Water is also dark and deep. So, when it is unbalanced, it can become turbulent and lose direction like Samudra. Apa tattva teaches us how to be reflective, flexible, and adaptable too. Even though Samudra mastered Apa, he could not control his greed and he lost his ability to reflect on his own actions. Water affects all our lives and senses too. Now, do you understand the power of water? Mastering Apa vidya means balancing its healing as well as destructive qualities." Tisva was impressed but he asked again, "Sir, don't you think all this is too much for me?" Danu nodded his head, "Dear boy, you need to grow up. The next time I visit you, be ready for a duel," Saying so he left.

It was already dawn. Vapih and Tisva got ready and went to school. The whole day, Tisva was lost in thoughts about the fight. He wondered whether he was ready for it. He started training more intensely because of which he spent less time with his family. He often wondered how his family would react when they would know about his secret.

Back at Aither, Samudra gave extra responsibilities to Danu and instructed him to report every night. Danu became terribly busy. His first visit to Tisva was successful, but he was unable to teleport again. One day, Danu requested Samudra for a day off, saying that he was unwell. Samudra agreed but was doubtful. Danu requested his friends to cover for him and left to meet Tisva.

Tisva had prepared well. At last, Danu arrived and so began the duel. Initially, it was friendly and mild. Slowly it turned intense. There was thunder and lightning. The wind was blowing crazily. It was frightening and destructive. Tisva was on the winning side but was destroying nature. Vapih interfered and together with Danu they calmed down the young master. After the fight, Tisva looked around and cried, "What did I do? "Danu tried to calm him and said, "You are ready now, but remember, *the power of water is in its balance. An ocean is made up of tiny droplets of water. Additionally, the power of a massive ocean can be contained in a single droplet, and you are that droplet.*" He left immediately.

The boy was tired. He went home and slept as Vapih watched him. The duel was indeed very intense. Samudra being a great warrior could sense that energy. He got alerted.

Chapter 10

DROPLET

Tisva ran a fever. The experience of the duel made him sick. He was tired and afraid.

Meanwhile, an alerted Samudra used his energy to learn about the duel. He got furious and called for Danu. He shouted, "How dare you trick me!? Who was that boy with you!?" Without any fear, Danu said, "He is the boy born out of the ring you wanted so desperately. He is a droplet of purity! He will soon punish you." Samudra paused for a second, and then laughed, "Ha-ha-ha-ha! That boy! Can he defeat me? I am an invincible wave. Nobody can even touch me." He locked Danu in the dungeons. There, Danu met Dhruti and Ravi. He informed them about the boy born out of the ring. Dhruthi spoke, "We are glad to know that the boy is ready. He will teach Samudra a lesson." "But, he is still not confident," said a concerned Danu.

Over time, Vapih and Tisva realized that Danu was captured by Samudra. Tisva uttered, "Now Samudra knows about me. He is waiting for me at Pancha-tattva-eka." Vapih replied, "Yes Tisva, you must act fast." However, Tisva was still not convinced that he could overpower the mighty Samudra. Once, Tisva woke up in the middle of the night. He was shivering with fear. Samudra had telepathically scared him.

The next day, Tisva did not go to school. He was not feeling well. He was walking in the fields with Vapih. The boys met someone there. He seemed to be a learned person. The man stopped them and spoke, "Dear son, I am Eka." Both the boys bowed in front of him. He continued, "Tisva, you are not an ordinary boy. You are the same boy who was born with the powers of the ring. You are divine. You are blessed with my virtues. So, if we put it correctly, you are my son and Samudra is your big brother. In addition, you absorbed the powers of all the warriors present around you that day." Tisva was dumbstruck. "You are tiny but stronger, and purer than Samudra. He has become evil in his greed. He needs to be punished. "Saying so, Eka caressed Tisva's forehead. Tisva felt some energy pass into him. He was confident now. Eka told him that apart from Apa tattva, Tisva had balanced his Pancha tattva too. He had powers from Druthi, the master of Prithvi and Apa tattva. Ravi gave him powers of justice and wisdom as he was the master of Agni and Akasha. Tisva received the gifts of controlling time and creating illusions from Laya who was the master of Shoonya Tattva. Ojas had given him the powers of Agni tattva. Finally, Tisva himself was the elixir of life just like Piyusha. Eka taught one final lesson, "Never forget your roots. You are the droplet of purity." With these words Eka encouraged Tisva. After a pause, Tisva spoke, "I am indeed blessed to be your child. I am extremely happy today. I will definitely teach my brother a lesson." Tisva then boldly when to his mother and grandparents. He told them about his secret and took their blessings.

He quickly teleported to Aither. As soon as he reached, Samudra was waiting for him. He had a huge army. Samudra spoke in a deep and heavy voice, "Welcome, welcome. I have been waiting for you." As he spoke, Tisva could hear huge waves gushing behind him. It was very frightening. Samudra was a terrible tide and Tisva was tiny. The army surrounded Tisva. Suddenly, he snapped his fingers, turned into water, and trickled off. Samudra mocked him, "The coward ran away, Hahaha…" Tisva trickled off into the dungeons of Pancha-tattva-eka and released his teacher Danu, Ravi, and Dhruti. He told them to prepare for the battle with Samudra's army. Suddenly, the tiny boy appeared in front of Samudra and challenged him face-to-face. An angry Samudra threw a huge tide at him. Before the boy could do anything he was washed away. However, a drenched Tisva stood up unharmed. Samudra aimed with bigger tides of water. This time, Tisva was prepared. He remembered his teacher's words and broke the waves into beautiful droplets of water. The droplets fell softly onto the ground, without hurting anyone.

Samudra was amazed and admired him but said, "Not so fast, now fight my ice crystals." Tisva suddenly saw many sharp ice crystals moving toward him at a great speed. He turned all of them into one big snowball and threw it back. Samudra was crushed by the snowball. Now, he was infuriated and started a huge storm with waves lashing everything. It was dangerous. Tisva closed his eyes and calmed himself. He had to protect the entire world from the devastating storm. He raised both his hands and sucked up all the storm into his palms and created a huge droplet. He threw it towards Samudra. Samudra got trapped inside it. He thought that he could easily break open the droplet but could not. Confused, he shouted, "why are my powers not working!?"

Tisva explained that the droplet was made of balanced Pancha tattva powers. Only the person who was balanced could break free. He said, "Dear brother, you will stay trapped in the droplet till the time you balance your own Pancha tattva."

Chapter 11

SUPERHERO

All the warriors thanked Tisva. Using the calming virtues of water, Tisva turned all the robust and wild fish back into cheerful ones. Upon his request, Dhruthi restored Aither back to its original serenity. Tisva declared Ravi as the king of Aither. Everyone requested Tisva to stay back but he nodded and said, "Eka told me never to forget my roots. If I stay here, I may become another Samudra, so, I want to go back to my sweet and humble family." Danu said, "Tisva, we will not stop you. You can help people wherever you are." Tisva firmly replied, "Yes sir." He hugged Danu and Vapih and bid them goodbye. He promised that he would stay connected with everyone and often visit them.

Back at home, Tisva was exhausted. He was relaxing on his bed when Sarita entered his room. She said, "Good, you are back. That means my tiny droplet punished Samudra. Vapih left a gift for you," saying so, she kept a box in the room and left him alone. Tisva opened the box and found a sea-blue colour suit. As he unfolded it, he got ecstatic. He screamed in excitement, "Awesome! This is what I wanted." It was a superhero suit equipped with nanotechnology. There was a pearly droplet symbol embossed on it. When he touched it, it felt completely like real water. As soon as he wore the suit, an eye mask appeared on his face with a screen. It was mind-blowing as all of it was made of liquid crystalline water. Then, he saw a folded piece of paper in the box, he opened the paper and read…..

"GO SAVE THE WORLD"

GO SAVE THE WORLD!!!

Glossary

(In The Order Of Appearance)

Tisva- Dewdrop

Sarita- River

Danu- related to water, flow.

Pancha-tattva-eka- Union of the five elements

Panchatattva- the five elements

Apa vidya- knowledge of water

Vidyalaya- A place of learning like a school

Aither- A personification of upper sky or space where gods reside

Eka- one, union

Agni/Anal- Fire

Prithvi- Earth

Anil/Vayu- Air

Akasha- sky

Shoonya- Space

Vapih- Pond or a water body

Tattva eka- Union of elements

Dhyana- focus, an initial step of meditation

Pranayama- disciplined breathing

Ojas- Energy

Mudras- gestures made by hands and fingers

Dhruthi- Determination

Ravi- Sun

Samudra- Ocean

Laya- Rhythm

Piyusha- Elixir of life

Pancha ratna- Five gemstones representing each of the five elements

Nanotechnology- Advanced science that deals with things in the nano-dimension.

Liquid crystalline water- fourth state of water where the properties are between liquid and solid.

www.ingramcontent.com/pod-product-compliance
Lightning Source LLC
LaVergne TN
LVHW061604070526
838199LV00077B/7165